Santi

I0390794

Brandon Joseph Park

For Those That Made My Life Beautiful

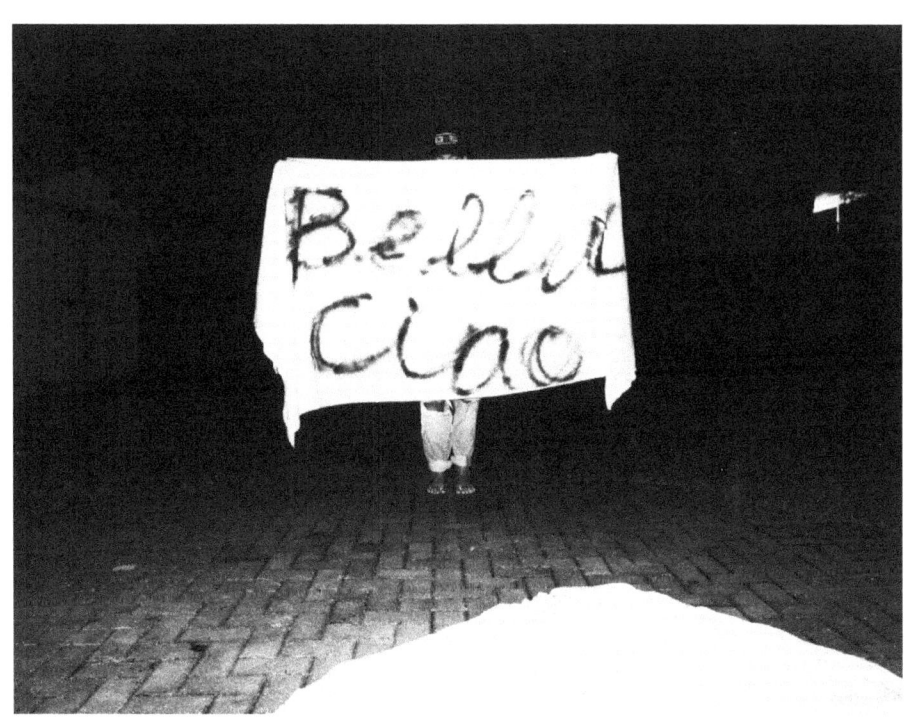

For You

I. Stories About Living

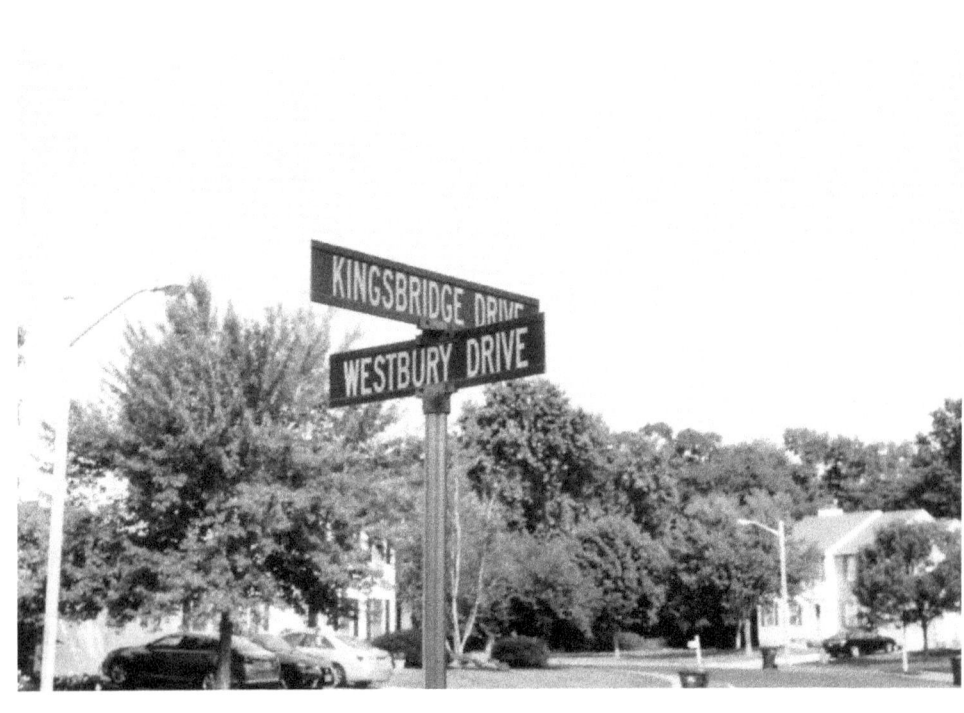

Westbury

It was four in the morning and Paul was waiting on his porch. He used to do this as a kid. It wouldn't be four in the morning, but he would wait on his porch as the other kids came running out of their houses. Paul lived in front of the street sign so everyone knew which house was his. That's where the school bus would arrive, so all the kids on the street would meet below it. Paul hated that everyone came together outside of his house, so he waited on his porch until the bus came, then he would run and be the last one on.
The truck honked and Paul grabbed his gloves and ran to get on.

"Morning, chief" he said.

The truck made its way around the neighborhood. It stopped at every house and Paul would jump out and do his job. It was like this every other Wednesday.

"Did you hear about the two brothers down the street?"

The chief finally spoke up.

"They went and killed someone. Drugs, I heard. They were selling or buying, I'm not sure. Either way something happened and they had to bury the body in their backyard. Cops got a call and you can imagine the rest. Crazy that that'd happen in this town, huh?"

He didn't know what to say. He knew them. The kids that did the killing. They were getting close to the house and he had to jump out to grab the garbage and throw it into the rear of the truck.

He stood there as the truck processed the trash. He knew them and here he was taking their mess. For once, he didn't feel like this was his town.

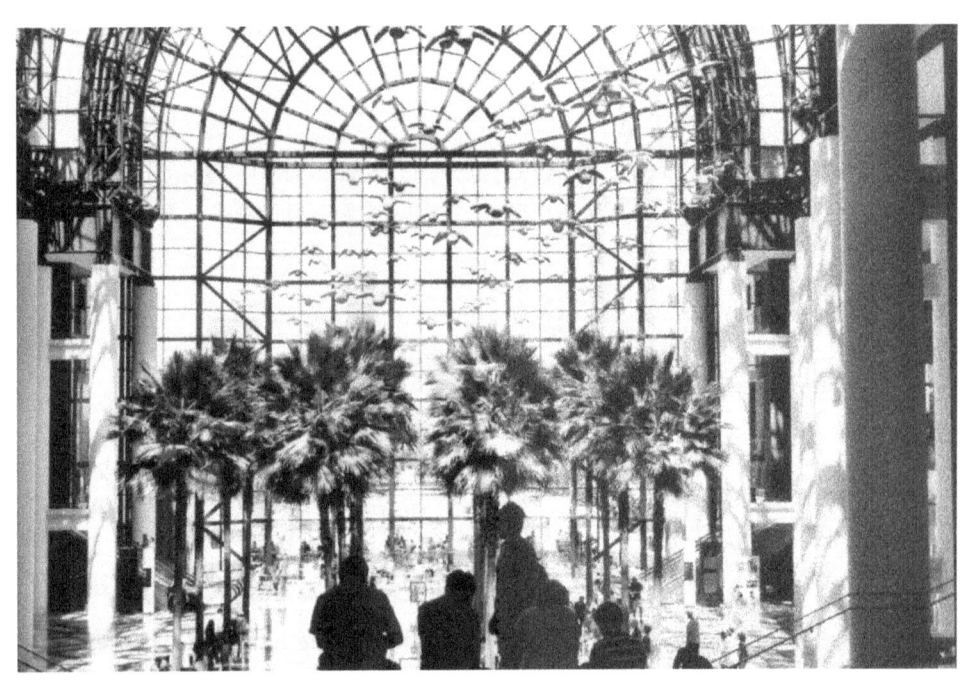

Fake

He liked to tell her little facts from his classes whenever they met. They didn't meet that often, so he always had something to say.

"Did you know that sunflowers will always face the sun when they bloom? It's because of photosynthesis or something. My teach explained it, but I sort of forgot" he said.

"You know, if you're gonna give me a trivia question, you should know the information" she said as she adjusted herself in her seat. They were sat in his car, parked in the lot of the local farm.

"All I know is that the sun makes the sunflowers grow so they know to face the sun and they can grow really big. Jeez, I was just trying to tell you something interesting." He said. He wanted to turn on the radio because now he felt dumb and he couldn't think of anything that could make himself sound smart.

He had to break it himself. The silence. But for some reason he couldn't think of anything he learned the day before or the day before that.

Nothing.

She kept fidgeting. He could tell she wanted to leave.

"You know, it doesn't help if you squirm around like that"

So they sat there, neither of them moving. The engine was on and it was loud.

It was keeping them quiet.

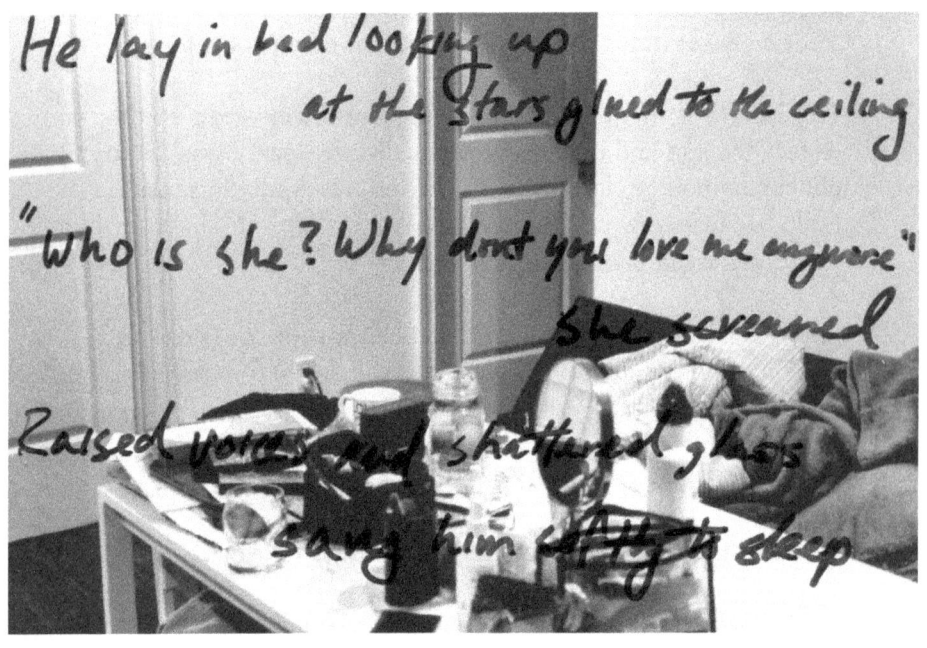

He lay in bed looking up
        at the stars glued to the ceiling

"Who is she? Why dont you love me anymore"
                            she screamed

Raised voices and shattered glass
        sang him softly to sleep

Stars

He lay in bed looking up at the stars glued to the ceiling

"Who is she? Why don't you love me anymore" she screamed

Raised voices and shattered glass sang him softly to sleep

They say that it was three of them

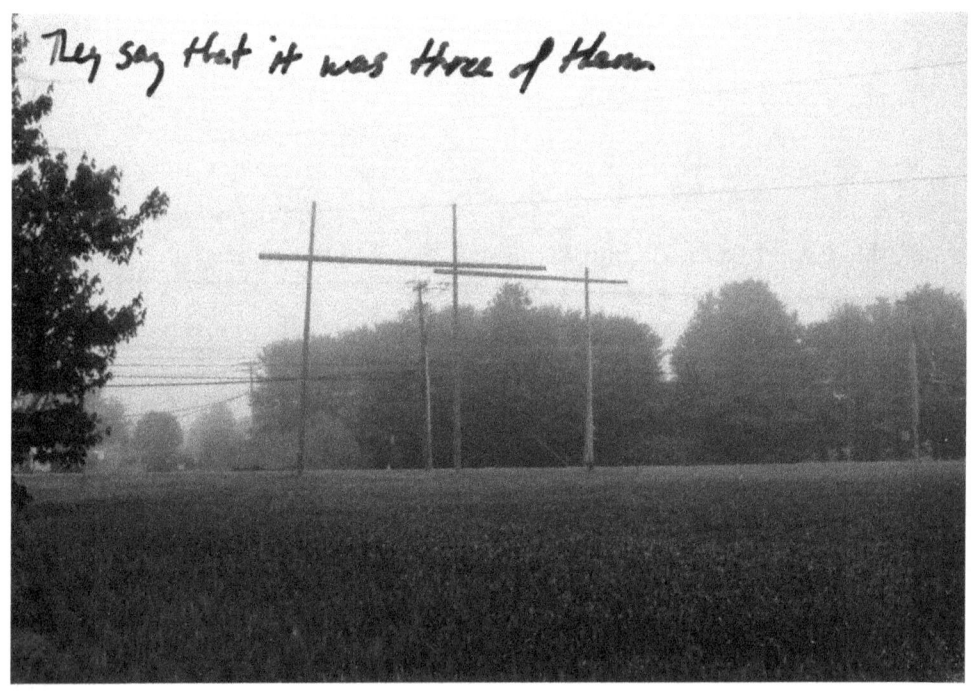

The Penitent Thief

I heard John pause at the break in the stairs. He usually takes the stairs two steps at a time. But this time he waited. He probably didn't know what to say to me. I can't blame him.

John took his seat next to me in the attic. We were facing the windows. I tried to break the silence.

"Ya know, it sorta looks like Golgotha up here"

"Come again?"

"Where Jesus was crucified. There were three crosses on that hill. I don't know why, but I always pictured these windows to be those crosses. Guess that makes me a thief. Guess that makes us the thieves"

"Yeah"

John handed me the bottle he brought from the kitchen. Neither of us had the time to pour it into a cup, so we took turns, passing it back and forth. I kept rambling.

"It's fitting, huh? Us two on the sides and him in the middle. It's weird because I don't even think about religious stuff like that. I can't seem to think about anything else but the things that remind me of him"

"Come on, not now..."

"You know, he'd want us to cry. I know you've been hiding it John. He'd want us to. It's okay to cry."

John got up and took the bottle. He was behind me now. I heard his footsteps.

"Honestly, All I've been doing is crying" I couldn't tell if John could hear me. I didn't know if he was even trying to listen. I kept talking just to make sure he heard.

"So I've been thinking, I'm gonna go through with that tattoo. Do you remember? We all wanted the same thing. He put up a fuss because he could never be seen with matching tattoos with his best friends. I'm gonna get it, John. Obviously you're free to join me"

His footsteps stopped. I didn't want to turn around. I traced the spot on my arm, where I would immortalize him. I stretched the skin. Maybe I could fit some more here. He wouldn't want me to dedicate a whole arm to him, he was never that selfish. It was starting to get warm so I knew I was getting drunk.

"You can't just not talk to me John. Let me know that you're still here with me man. You're not the only one dealing with this shit, he was my friend too."

I heard him come back. He sat down and handed me the bottle. I couldn't look him in the eyes. I looked down and reached out for the bottle. His shoes were wet, maybe he spilled. I took a sip and took another one right after. I motioned for John to take the bottle back. He finally spoke.

"How could he just leave us? Now we have to finish this fucking bottle by ourselves"

He let the bottle slip out of his hands and break against the floor. For some reason, I told John the truth.

"Lately, I've been thinking about calling it quits too. Go out the same way he did, not even tell anyone, just a short letter to my parents, that's it. I don't believe in God but maybe I'd get to see him again. Like in some special place for cowards. And I'll be greeted by him and we can talk again."

I heard John crying. I looked up for the first time and saw his face. I saw him crying. He was looking out the window again, I've never seen him cry before. His mouth was moving, but nothing was coming out. I turned away, because I couldn't take looking at him like this. I tried to find what he was looking at through the window. Maybe he wasn't looking at anything. Then I heard him say it.

"Don't leave me alone"

II. Stories About Loving

Let's Talk About Love

"Do you think we were just destined to meet some people?"

"Can you be a little more specific?"

I could tell that Mike didn't know what I was talking about. When this happens, he just chalks it up to the alcohol and listens to me. I get away with saying some stupid stuff.

"Haven't you ever seen someone and asked yourself, where the fuck have you been all my life..."

"I'm a bit more observant than you, bud. I tend to acknowledge other people, I don't have my head up my ass like you do."

Mike was not getting what I was trying to tell him.

"Can't you tell? I'm in love, man. I finally talked to her and she was everything I thought she'd be."

"What's this have to do with destiny?"

Mike did not like where I was going with this.

"Who are we talking about anyways?"

"Well, this girl, her names Allison. I swear to god she just appeared in my class. I'm positive that I've never seen her before, you know I'm always checking out the girls. I asked the guy next to me and he says that Allison has been in class since the fall! I nearly lost it. Are you really trying to tell me that I didn't notice this drop dead gorgeous girl all semester? That's what I mean by destiny, Mike. Let me tell you, I've never fallen so hard for a girl in all my life. And to think she was sitting a few seats ahead of me this entire time! Somebody wanted me to notice her and somebody wanted me to fall in love, that just has to be the case"

"Sounds like you're just a dick that couldn't give two shits about his classmates. You just picked out the prettiest girl in your class and fell in love?" Mike ordered another round because he could tell where this was headed.

Mike has been with me since freshman year. We got stuck in the same remedial English course, and let me tell you, it was like being sentenced to hell. Obviously we got close because of that, and we've been drinking partners ever since. He's trying to be a surgeon or something, so I like to think of him as the realist in this partnership.

"Mike, have you ever seen me like this before? This time it's different. I don't care if you think I'm vain or call me an asshole for this, I'm determined to make it happen"

"I thought you said you believed in destiny? If it's really your destiny to be with this girl, you can just sit back and wait for everything to fall into place, right?"

"Wrong. It's been two months since that day I saw her in class. Ever since then I've been like a fucking peacock shaking my dumb rainbow colored ass trying to find a mate. I couldn't wait any longer. So, for once in my life, I fucking went for it."

As I said that, I put out my hand. Scribbled on it was a phone number in black ink.

"Wow I'm actually impressed. How'd you pull that off?"

"As cool as I've sounded up until this point, you're gonna have a laugh at this. So I brought my SLR to class, obviously with the intention of making myself seem artsy and sensitive. After class was dismissed, I waited for her to leave and then I chased after her. I acted like I was out of breath, ya know, to make it seem urgent or whatever. I introduced myself and told her that I'm an aspiring artist. I said that she would be the perfect model for my next project. Shut the fuck up, stop laughing. Anyways, she was flattered and I threw out some 'you're the prettiest girl I've met' bullshit and she said yes. I asked if we could set a day to shoot so she gave me her number and told me to call whenever I wanted."

"Wow you're a real Casanova, let me tell you. But seriously, good work, I never would've expected this kind of move outta you"

Mike got us a shot of rum to celebrate. I was on top of the world.

"So what's part two of this grand scheme to make Allison fall in love with you?"

"I think the first step would be to learn how to use this damn camera, then we can talk about love"

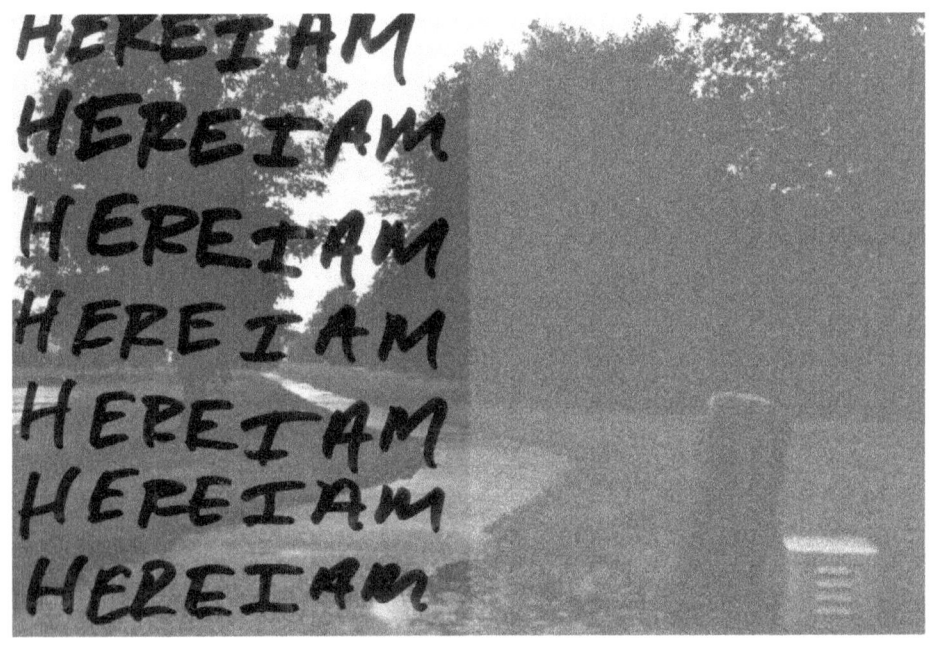

Broken Bones

She was a few steps ahead of me. She liked to lead the way, so I let her choose how we'd get to the bar this time. She took us the back way, maybe because it's a Thursday night, maybe because she got lost. I never know with her. Either way, nobody would be able to see us enter together.

We sat in the booth in the corner. It was far enough away from the jukebox that we could speak without screaming and close enough to the door that we could feel the breeze when drunks left for the night.

"We can't see each other anymore" She said in a low voice.

"But why?"

"Because he'll kill you " She said "and he won't be afraid to do it"

I sat back in my chair.

"If you're so sure, tell him to come get me, I'm wide open"

I threw my arms up wildly.

"But he won't take you seriously" She said quietly as she shifted in her seat.

"What's that supposed to mean? I'll make him take me seriously"

"I could seriously lose you" She said.

"I don't get why you're with him in the first place. Don't you want something special? Where serious doesn't matter and being quiet means nothing?"

"If I told you" She said "You'd have me too easily".
It was then that I felt the wind against my face and I heard him yell my name over the sounds of the jukebox.

Boys BREAK the Beautiful
Boys BREAK the Beautiful
Boys BREAK the Beautiful
Boys BREAK the Beau
Boys BREAK th
Boys BRE
Boys

The Buzz of the Neon

Chris has been asking me to come along on dates with him and his girlfriend, Sara. Hell, he might as well have been begging me. Just from the look on his face, I knew that something was wrong with the relationship. He knew it and I knew it.

"I swear it'll only be one night, maybe a couple of hours. Just enough time for me to get drunk and then you can leave. I'll be able to handle it once I'm drunk."

To be honest, I didn't owe Chris any favors. He's the kind of friend that can't help but get a flat at 2 in the morning. He's always been a bit helpless, so our friendship has been built around just that; help. "Fine. Only a few beers and I'm gone. You're buying."

We talked about it in the car. He told me that he read Sara's diary when she was gone. Something about running away and starting over again. Sounded to me like a hit and run, and Chris was just another name on Sara's list. But Chris insisted that he was the one making her unhappy. He said that he can't even have a conversation with her without stumbling over his words. He said that he wanted to try and impress her or make himself seem worth something, but all he could do was waste her time with the stuttering.

I don't blame him for being this paranoid. He was just getting over a divorce when he met Sara. He liked her pretty body and young face. She liked his money. I warned him about her, but he chose not to listen to me. He said he wanted something dangerous in his life. We got to the bar and Sara was waiting at the door. I introduced myself to her, and she greeted me with a smile. I told them that I was gonna have a cigarette before going in. She turned and grabbed onto Chris's arm and they walked ahead into the bar.

I didn't have any smokes. I thought about whether to leave or stay. I didn't know what was keeping me there in the first place. And so I stood, alone in front of the bar with the buzz of the neon "open" sign, the only thing on my mind.

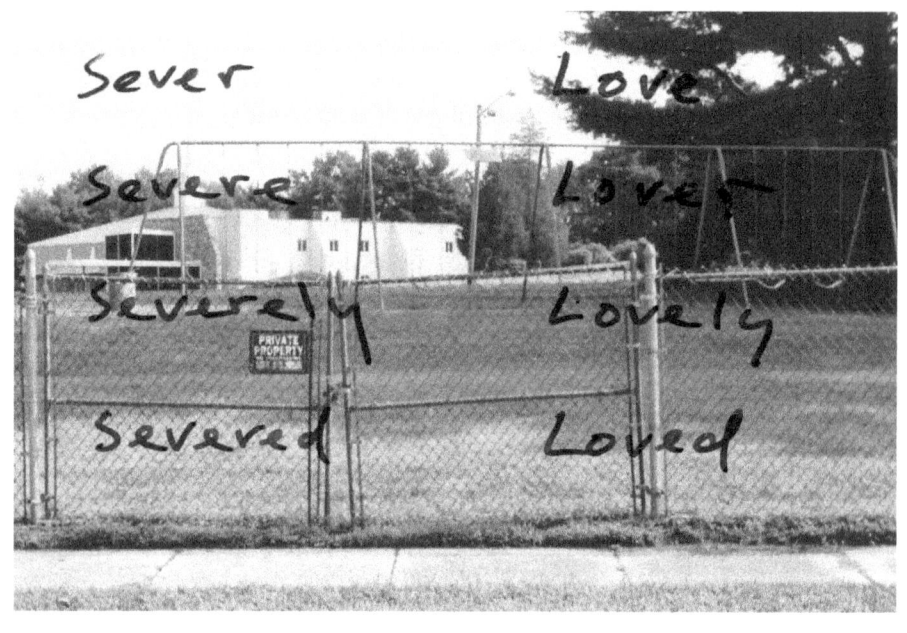

What We Miss While We're Falling In Love

Jenny was married to a man she did not love. She was 24 and afraid that he would get in the way.

"I'll be home late tonight, honey. Work."

She put down the receiver. It didn't matter which one of them said it. They took turns hiding. She dialed another number.

"Can you come over tonight? I made some tea, so get here before it gets cold"

There was a time that she loved him. They were young then, and he promised her a lot. He promised her a house, a car, money. She always thought it was funny how she could never call him a liar because everything came true. He wasn't a liar. She just wished he promised her happiness.

The doorbell rang and she undid her hair. She waited a second, to hide the fact that she was sitting on the stairs waiting. She opened the door and it was Ryan. Ryan was a mechanic and he was happy.

"Thanks for coming, Ryan. I just can't stand being in this goddamn house alone"

"I hope I didn't get here too late, it's fucking freezing in that garage and I could use some tea"

They headed into the kitchen. He led the way. He took his seat at the table and Jenny went to the find a pair of mugs. She poured the hot water and dropped in a bag of tea into each. She placed the mug in front of Ryan and took her seat.

"So, how's the engine holding up? I've been busy, I'm sorry I haven't had the chance to get to work on it."

"It's just fine. Don't you get tired of talking about cars and engines? Let's talk about something else"

She used a spoon to stir her tea. Sometimes she forgets to let it steep. Sometimes she keeps it in for too long.

"Have you ever thought about going out to sea? You know, in a small sailboat. Maybe big enough to fit two people. You ever think about that?"

Jenny was panicking at this point. She wanted to take back what she just said. She couldn't stop thinking about how stupid she sounded.

"No, I get sea sick. Anyways, sailboats don't have an engine, I'd have no clue what to do. I don't like the idea of being left to the wind. I don't want it to choose where I'm going. It's sort of like yelling to God that you're unhappy with the life he gave you and you're gonna leave the rest up to nature"

"Hmmm, I guess you're right. You would be pretty useless. You're uninvited to my adventure"

Jenny kept stirring her tea. She took a sip and spit it back into the mug. The bag of tea broke. She slid the mug to the side.

"Hey, back in the day they would read the bottoms of teacups. You know, see where the leaves would settle and try and see pictures in the tea. I'd sort of do that as a kid. I'd have my alphabet soup and just drink the broth. I'd get to the bottom and only the letters would be left. I always wanted to find something written there for me. See something in all the disorder, that sort of thing. It never worked out though, all the letters were in different directions. Like an upside down W or a sideways Z. I guess if I think about it now, there really wasn't a way to tell what was upside down and right side up, huh? It would just look like an M anyways."

Jenny didn't hear anything past the part about the tea. She was staring into her mug, trying to make sense of the mess she made.